Standish O'Grady

THE IRISH WRITERS SERIES

James F. Carens, General Editor

STANDISH O'GRADY

by
Phillip L. Marcus

Lewisburg
BUCKNELL UNIVERSITY PRESS

© 1970 by Associated University Presses, Inc.
Library of Congress Catalogue Card Number: 74-124647

Associated University Presses, Inc.
Cranbury, New Jersey 08512

ISBN: 8387-7751-1 cloth
8387-7660-4 paper
Printed in the United States of America

Contents

CONTENTS

Preface

Standish James O'Grady is one of the most important but least known figures in modern Irish literature. No less an authority than W. B. Yeats was to write that "I think it was his 'History of Ireland, Heroic Period,' that started us all," and while this was an exaggeration O'Grady's central position is shown by the long list of other writers who acknowledged his influence, among them Katherine Tynan, John Todhunter, T. W. Rolleston, and Aubrey de Vere. Another early contemporary, AE (George Russell), declared that "whatever is Irish in me he kindled to life," and many years later O'Grady's power was still strong enough to be felt by Austin Clarke. Yet his work, which never did attain a very wide circulation, is today extremely scarce, difficult to find in even the best libraries, and seldom read, while in the area of critical attention there is no full-length study of his writing, and only a few scattered essays. This disparity between his significance and the quantity of serious criticism would alone demand a new consideration of that work. But O'Grady's books—at least the best of them—are not of merely antiquarian interest, but possess substantial interest and merit as literature. It is thus all the more important that he should be better known, and the purpose of this study is to help make him so. While the focus of the study is not primarily biographical, the books themselves are discussed in their personal and historical settings, and O'Grady's place in the evolution of the "Irish Renaissance" is also assessed. In combination these perspectives will, I trust, make it clear that he deserves a personal renaissance.

The Life and Work of Standish James O'Grady: a Chronology
(1846 – 1928)

(Biographical information about O'Grady is scarce and inclined to be imprecise; consequently it has been necessary in a few instances to estimate approximate dates.)

1846: O'G. born, County Cork, Ireland

1868: receives B.A. from Trinity College, Dublin

1872: called to the Bar

1873-1877: begins writing on literary subjects; becomes affiliated with the Dublin *Daily Express*; undergoes a conversion to *Irish* interests

1878: *History of Ireland: The Heroic Period* published

1879: *Early Bardic Literature, Ireland*

1880: *History of Ireland: Cuculain and his Contemporaries*

1881: *History of Ireland: Critical and Philosophical;* becomes involved in Irish land problems

1882: *The Crisis in Ireland; Cuculain: An Epic*

1886: *Toryism and the Tory Democracy*

1889: *Red Hugh's Captivity*

1892: *Finn and His Companions*

1893: *The Bog of Stars*

1894: *The Coming of Cuculain; The Story of Ireland*

1896: *In the Wake of King James; Ulrick the Ready*

1897: *The Flight of the Eagle*

1898: *All Ireland*; at about this time, leaves the *Daily Express* to take up the editorship of the *Kilkenny Moderator*

1900: founds and edits *All Ireland Review*

1901: *In the Gates of the North*

1902: *Hugh Roe O'Donnell*

1907: gives up editorship of *All Ireland Review; The Masque of Finn*

1918: leaves Ireland permanently for health reasons

1920: *The Triumph and Passing of Cuculain*

1928: dies, Isle of Wight

Standish O'Grady

1.
O'Grady and Ancient Ireland

Standish O'Grady was born in 1846 at Castletown, Berehaven, in the County Cork, the son of a Protestant clergyman and small landowner. After completion of his studies at Tipperary Grammar School he matriculated at Trinity College, Dublin, where he compiled a brilliant record before graduation in 1868. Too independent in mind to pursue the clerical career for which he had been destined, he chose to study the Law and was called to the Bar in 1872. He contributed some literary articles to the *Gentlemen's Magazine* and did lead-writing for the Dublin *Daily Express*. To this point his career was similar to that of many other promising young men of the "Ascendancy" (the predominantly Protestant and Unionist Irish upper class), and he might well have gone through his life remaining, like them, in his country but not of it, an Irishman who knew nothing of Irish history and tradition and believed that whatever history and tradition there might be were beneath contempt. The T.C.D. curriculum contained no consideration of indigenous subjects, and O'Grady's masters and acquaintances shared his ignorance. He himself even knew personally Sir Samuel Ferguson (one of the few contemporary members of the Ascendancy who *was* in touch with the national heritage) without being made aware by anyone that he was "a great Irish poet." In the days of O'Grady's youth the "Anglicization" of Ireland, the intentional destruction of native culture that had been initiated centuries earlier as a device for crushing resistance to English rule, was almost complete: neither the Young Ireland movement of the 1840s nor the Fenian movement of the 1860s had succeeded in reversing the tide. Fortunately, O'Grady's own position was changed through a chance discovery of one of the few counterforces in operation at that time, changed so radically that he himself was eventually to play a major role in what Douglas Hyde termed the "de-Anglicizing" of Ireland, the resurrection of Gaelic culture and the continued growth of a national consciousness.

O'Grady seems to have been about 27 or 28 years old at the time of the crucial encounter. (By his own later recollections his age was 23, but this would seem to place the event too early.) While staying at a country house in the West of Ireland he was forced by bad weather to remain indoors, and in the library of the house happened upon a three-volume history of Ireland by Sylvester O'Halloran—the first history of his country into which he had ever looked. Though impassioned concerning his subject, O'Halloran was also rational and scholarly, and O'Grady was impressed; how, he wondered, had all this interesting material never been brought to his attention? Determined to learn more, he went upon his return to Dublin to the Royal Irish Academy, and soon he was deep in research. His most important discovery was the works of the great Gaelic scholar Eugene O'Curry, in whose encyclopedic compilations *Lectures on the Manuscript Materials of Ancient Irish History* and *Manners and Customs of the Ancient Irish* he met for the first time Ireland's rich store of heroic literature. That literature became the greatest formative influence upon his personal worldview and the books he himself was to write. He suddenly saw that he had been the victim of a grievous illusion: his country not only had an indigenous tradition, but a tradition that one could be proud of and inspired by. In fact, no country in Europe had a more glamorous and impressive body of epic materials, and only in Greece was there anything even comparable. Determined that others would not remain in the same state of ignorance that he had endured, he began to write his own history of Ireland (*History of Ireland,* Volume One, *The Heroic Period;* Volume Two, *Cuculain and His Contemporaries*); he completed it between 1878 and 1880 and published it at his own expense, as there was no contemporary market for such subjects. This unimpressive looking work, which fell from the presses almost stillborn, was soon to be diligently sought and reverently studied and quoted by the young men and women who collectively constituted the "Irish Renaissance."

The material with which O'Grady was working falls

into three major categories. In the first of these are all
legends involving the Tuatha Dé Danann (Tribes of
the Goddess Danu), thought to have been the gods of
the ancient Irish, and other early groups supposed to
have invaded Ireland. The second category, often called
the Red Branch Cycle, deals with heroes treated as
having lived in what is now Ulster at about the beginning of the Christian Era. Chief figures in this cycle
include Conchobor, King of the Ulidians; Fergus
MacRóig, who had been king until ousted by Conchobor; and above all Cú Chulainn, the greatest warrior
of the Red Branch. The most important event in this
cycle is the Cattle-drive of Cualnge, in which the northern province is attacked and pillaged by forces from all
the other provinces of Ireland under the leadership of
Medb, Queen of Connaught and Fergus MacRóig, who
has defected from the Ulster side. At the time of the
invasion all of the Red Branch heroes except Cú Chulainn are overcome by a mysterious malady that
deprives them of their faculties, and thus he has to
defend the province alone. He does so successfully,
though in the process he has to kill his boyhood friend
Fer Diad and is very seriously wounded himself. Another portion of this cycle is the famous tale of Deirdre
(the Irish Helen of Troy) and the Sons of Usnach.
The central concern of the third category is the exploits
of the Fianna, a kind of Irish militia, and of its leader,
Fionn MacCumhaill. The events of this cycle are traditionally placed in the third century, during the reign
of the historical monarch Cormac MacArt. (The degree
of historicity in all three of these groups of legends is

a subject of continuing debate.) O'Grady's imagination
was moved most powerfully by the Cú Chulainn story,
and it was this which comprised the central concern of
the *History*; he was, however, strongly interested in
the other two groups as well and eventually gave them
fuller treatment, the gods in his *History of Ireland:
Critical and Philosophical* and the Fianna in *Finn and
His Companions*.

O'Grady's task in trying to make these legends better
known was a more difficult one than the above scheme
might suggest, for they did not come to him in any
such neat arrangement. The old stories in fact survived
not in a single, unified fabric, but rather in a myriad
of fragments. Many of the individual stories were in-
complete and often there might be several variant
versions of a single tale. Further confusion came from
textual corruption and from modifications intentionally
introduced by clerical copyists, who brought in anach-
ronistic Christian elements and sought to obliterate
evidence of "paganism" by euhemerizing the old Irish
gods. Nor was there any formal harmony in the old
texts, which were a jumble of prose and verse, epics,
lyrics, pseudo-histories, genealogies and other miscel-
laneous kinds of writing. Finally there was the language
problem: the stories were preserved primarily in Middle
Irish, and even by the second half of the nineteenth
century English translations were relatively few and
difficult to obtain. There was not even a single published rendering of the entire story of the Cattle-drive
of Cualnge (the *Táin Bó Cúalnge*) and thus O'Grady,
who could not read Irish, had to rely primarily upon

a manuscript translation which a later and more accomplished Gaelic scholar has termed "wretched." Proof of the virtual chaos with which O'Grady was confronted is found in the fact that he originally assumed that the Fenian Cycle should *precede* the Red Branch Cycle and then in the second volume of the *History* had to confess his error.

These extremely difficult conditions raised the further issue of precisely how faithful to the received materials one must be in presenting them to modern audiences. One possible alternative was the absolute faithfulness of the scholar, which had the obvious disadvantage of sacrificing appeal to many general readers. A second course might involve turning into verse or "literary" prose the literal rendering of a scholarly translation, but the blurring of aesthetic virtues in the form and organization of most of the surviving tales constituted a serious drawback to this approach. A method yet more likely to appeal to a broad audience while even less faithful to the sources would be to use a literary medium and also to impose an aesthetically satisfactory form. To make the subject matter into a "good story" might involve altering the genre of the original, changing the plot by combining different versions and omitting or even adding elements, and elaborating and making consistent the characterizations. The author using this approach would have to stress his concern with faithfulness to the "spirit" of his sources. While a few other writers (notably Ferguson) had used the legendary materials before O'Grady, no one approach had been clearly validated; consequently he had to solve this problem himself, and he found himself attracted by the polar extremes of scholarly respect and imaginative improvement.

As a child O'Grady had been conditioned by two powerful forces: the wild natural surroundings of his home on the southern coast and the rigorous academic training he received at the Tipperary Grammar School. It is perhaps not overly fanciful to see these forces behind the complex response to the legendary materials revealed in the *History of Ireland* and his later books on the subject. The very title of the *History* seemed to reveal a definite stand, but that definiteness was belied immediately by the introduction to the 1878 volume. There O'Grady used the term "archaeology" to cover what in his time would ordinarily have been considered "history": that discipline which treats the past "in a rigid and conscientious spirit," the "accumulation of names, dates, events, disquisitions, the balancing of probabilities, the testing of statements and traditions, categorical assertions concerning laws and customs." "In history," on the other hand, "there must be sympathy, imagination, creation." In the terminology O'Grady used in this passage, the findings of "archaeology" are the raw materials with which the "historian" works: he will study them intently, "after which, in proportion to his strength and truth of imagination, a more or less faithful and vivid picture of that life of which they are the relics, will impress itself on his mind." Here the latent tension for O'Grady between the scholarly and the imaginative was held in check by the device of referring to the latter by a name traditionally associated with the former.

At once, however, he began to vacillate. No sooner

had he criticized the seventeenth-century Irish chroni-
cler Geoffrey Keating for giving only the bare bones
of the old stories and neglecting the qualities in them
which O'Grady himself most valued, "the epic and
dramatic," than he lamented the impossibility (because
of the chaotic condition in which they had been preserved) of reproducing *all* the surviving texts in the
sort of vast scholarly compendium for which O'Curry
had hoped. Then a further attempt at synthesis:
O'Grady announced his own method as "the reduction
to its artistic elements of the whole of that heroic
history taken together, viewing it always in the light
shed by the discoveries of modern archaeologians, frequently using the actual language of the bards, and as
much as possible their style and general character of
expression." The phrase "reduction to its artistic elements" is a clear statement of the "good story" approach.
But the text of the *History* itself proved not to fall
entirely within that category: it began with fifty pages
of "archaeological" material concerning the background
of the story. Furthermore, in 1879 O'Grady published
the monograph *Early Bardic Literature* in which he
apologized for the "failures" in the approach adopted
in the first volume of the *History*. He had not made it
clear enough that his material was "absolutely historic":
his narrative seemed to "progress too much in the air,
too little in time and space," to be "more in the nature
of legend and romance than of actual historical fact
seen through an imaginative medium." He confessed
that "the blaze of bardic light which illuminates those
centuries at first so dazzled the eye and disturbed the

judgment, that I saw only the literature, only the epic and dramatic interest, and did not see as I should the distinctly historical character of the age around which that literature revolves. . . ." He promised that the second volume would "remedy that defect." *Early Bardic Literature* in fact became the first 88 pages of that second volume, and incorporated along with these apologetic remarks a substantial additional quantity of "archaeological" material. From that point, however, the epic narrative was resumed in essentially the same mode as it had been treated in Volume One, except for the addition of a large number of footnotes giving references to scholarly sources. Thus in both volumes an "archaeological" section was followed by a longer "historical" one.

The balance achieved by combining these elements within the same covers was a decidedly perilous one, and broke down very rapidly. In 1881 O'Grady published the first (and as it turned out, the only) volume of a *History of Ireland: Critical and Philosophical* in which he proposed to treat the Irish past in a manner "critical, not constructive or imaginative." Several of the "archaeological" portions of the earlier *History* were transferred verbatim and most of the rest were reproduced in substance though greatly expanded in scope. Then in 1882 the "history" sections were combined in a single volume and published under the title *Cuculain: an Epic.* Still later he was to further revise this part of the original *History* into an almost novelistic trilogy. The division in O'Grady's sympathies was too great to be permanently closed.

The approach which O'Grady used in the imaginative portions of the *History* to reduce the corpus of legendary materials to its "artistic elements" was itself influenced by a combination of motives. Chief among these was his desire to present a glamorous and appealing image of the Irish heroic age, which he frankly idealized. Already some writers had used this new source of subject matter for less than elevated purposes: P. W. Joyce, writing in 1879, spoke critically of specimens "presented in a very unfavourable and unjust light—distorted to make them look *funny,* and their characters debased to the mere modern conventional stage Irishman." O'Grady, on the other hand, regarded "this age and the great personages moving therein as incomparably higher in intrinsic worth than the corresponding ages of Greece. In Homer, Hesiod, and the Attic poets, there is a polish and artistic form, absent in the existing monuments of Irish heroic thought, but the gold, the ore itself, is here massier and more pure, the sentiment deeper and more tender, the audacity and freedom more exhilarating, the reach of imagination more sublime, the depth and power of the human soul more fully exhibit themselves." He saw the period as one of unparalleled nobility and excitement: "Out of the ground start forth the armies of her demigods and champions—an age bright with heroic forms, loud with the trampling of armies and war-steeds, with the roar of chariot-wheels, and the shouting of warriors. . . ." For him Cú Chulainn's combat with Fer Diad was "the most profoundly tragic scene in all literature," and Cú himself "the noblest character."

Clearly this idealized vision of the heroic past of their country had much to do with the book's appeal to other Irish writers. AE's description of his own feelings when he first read O'Grady reveals that it was precisely this vision which moved him: the emotion was like that of a man "who suddenly feels ancient memories rushing at him, and knows he was born in a royal house, that he had mixed with the mighty of heaven and earth and had the noblest for his companions." Rolleston's reaction was similar: "The shadowy gods and warriors ceased to be mere names; they took heroic shape and form. They were filled with passions, terrific and superhuman sometimes, but profoundly moving. . . . This was the first book I ever read which convinced me that there was such a thing as a spiritual Ireland." However, while O'Grady's approach was effective, it was not really faithful even to the spirit of his originals.

Those originals are no more uniform in world-view than they are in style, and in them the heroic and noble are mixed with the comic, the fantastic, the coarse. Thus in the case of his central character, Cú Chulainn, O'Grady could not accept the descriptions of him as having three-colored hair (thought by some scholars to be a vestige of an original association of him with the sun), seven-colored pupils in each eye, and seven digits on each of his hands and feet, let alone his grotesque "distortions":

Then his first distortion came upon Cú Chulainn so that he became horrible, many-shaped, strange and unrecognisable. . . . He performed a wild feat of contortion with his body inside his skin. His feet and his shins and his knees came to the back; his heels and his calves and his hams came to the front. . . . Then his face became a red hollow [?]. He sucked one of his eyes into his head so that a wild crane could hardly have reached it to pluck it out from the back of his skull on to the middle of his cheek. The other eye sprang out on to his cheek. His mouth was twisted back fearsomely. . . . The hero's light rose from his forehead so that it was long and as thick as a hero's whetstone. As high, as thick, as strong, as powerful and as long as the mast of a great ship was the straight stream of dark blood which rose up from the very top of his head and became a dark magical mist like the smoke of a palace when a king comes to be attended to in the evening of a wintry day.

Similarly it was necessary for him to change the *ga bulga,* Cú Chulainn's invincible spear which had to be cast from between the toes and once within the body released a great number of barbs so that it could not be withdrawn, into a "rude spear" thrown in the ordinary manner.

In the "archaeological" section of the second volume of the *History* he asserted that "a noble moral tone pervades the whole" of the early literature. But this was plainly untrue, and as he himself admitted many years later, he found things in that literature which he "simply could not write down and print and publish," things reflecting "the very loose morality of the age." At the time of writing the *History* he tried to convince himself that most of the "ignoble" elements were not canonical, and that he was capable in each case of judging. One such element was the sexual liaisons between Fergus and Medb, which he omitted entirely.

Cú Chulainn's affairs with the amazon Aoife, who bore him his only son, Connla, and with his concubine Ethne Inguba were similarly unacceptable. In both of these cases O'Grady was not content merely to omit the offending incident: he felt compelled to provide substitutes. Thus he retained Cú Chulainn's son, but made his mother Emer, Cú's actual wife; and he added a scene showing Ethne as a child, fascinated by Cú when he visits the home of her family, and later referred to her as "a very dear friend" of Cú Chulainn.

In both of these latter incidents prudishness and the desire to preserve an idealized vision of the subject-matter are blended with a strong vein of sentimentality. Unable to resist the easy sentiment obtainable in literature from child characters, O'Grady not only fabricated the incident involving the childhood of Ethne, but also invented a younger offspring for Cú Chulainn, an infant named Fionscota, and several episodes involving the parental tenderness of the great warrior and the similar emotion of his charioteer Laeg. As today young boys are allowed to sit behind the wheel of the family car, so Connla was taken for a chariot ride and Laeg "entrusted the reins to his tiny hands." Most flagrantly of all, O'Grady introduced an elaborate scene depicting Cú and Laeg walking through the city of Dublin and looking in the shop-windows (!), where they saw a moving wooden model of a war chariot which Laeg, remembering the little child back home, bought as a present for him.

This scene is purely imaginary, having absolutely no precedent in the old texts. Nevertheless, O'Grady's motivation for including it was not entirely "imaginative." Though he must have known better about the shop-windows, he did believe that there was historical evidence of a thriving city on the site of what is now Dublin long before the date traditionally assigned for its founding, and he wanted to tie the events of the Cú Chulainn story to their "factual" background.

In the introduction to the first volume of the *History* O'Grady argued that it had been a convention among the early Irish bards to omit from their works all references to the more prosaic activities of the culture; although he himself claimed that such activities were now "sufficiently poetical," he was clearly responding to his more historical and scholarly impulses in determining to introduce "boldly the ancient civilization of the country": "in this part of my work I have preserved the closest adherence to the authorities. In all that relates to the material, social, political condition of the country, I believe that in this and in the succeeding volumes will be found an accurate and faithful representation of the civilization of ancient Ireland." The result was that the *History* is filled with such information, the greater part of it culled from O'Curry's *Manners and Customs*.

Volume One, for example, pauses in the progress of the narrative to devote four pages to the depiction of an Irish law court. Technical terms are used abundantly, and there is extensive detail about the structure of the court and the procedures of the trials. O'Grady tried to make this material seem more integral by "dramatizing" it—that is, treating it as an episode in the story—and involving in it a character from the main narrative. Nevertheless, the material diverts the story line, and produces a further negative effect because one of the trials upon which he focused was a particularly ludicrous one. It involved a harper who had been ordered by a drunken "*fudir*," a "base fellow," to play for him; but "the harper, not deeming it right to flatter a drunken beast, refused, and the other flung violently at him a housewife's spatula which chanced to be near, and smote him on the back of the right hand, and his hand was disabled for many days, and the nail had fallen from the thumb." Then, there being no defense in the case, "the Ard-ollav computed first the enechlan on account of the insult, and this was determined according to his rank, and after that the corp-diera for the wounding." At this point the character whose activities the narrative has been relating stepped forward and "begged to be permitted to repeat an ancient rann applicable to that case," and "when this was gladly granted, he repeated a verse of the laws of Fohla, compact and sure in the strong fetters of alliteration and assonance, according to which there was a special damage on account of the making of an artificial nail, to be fitted dextrously to the finger by a skilled person in order that the harper might return to the practice of his art the sooner." Such an episode hardly coincides with that heroic and noble picture of the early Irish period which O'Grady had taken such pains to create, and suggests a real inconsistency in his judgment. Not all of the interpolated scenes dealing with the institutions of the period are equally bathetic, and perhaps they do help achieve O'Grady's objective of giving solidity to the airy stuff of bardic romance (much airier when filtered through his imagination than in the old texts themselves), but their cumulative effect upon the narrative is to slow its forward thrust.

This last criticism leads to the larger question of just how O'Grady, conditioned by the complex of motives analyzed above, made the mass of legends dealing with the life of Cú Chulainn into a "good story"—not only what the characteristic features of his approach were, but also how *successful* he was in achieving his literary goal.

O'Grady's education had left him with a thorough knowledge of and a deep love for Classical literature, and it is consequently no surprise that when seeking a literary model for the form of his work he should turn to the epic. When he had the chance to reprint the book in 1882 without the "archaeological" chapters he could use the term "Epic" in his title, but only the name was new: the epic characteristics were there in the *History*. The choice of models was a good one. It has been suggested by some Celtic scholars that the *Táin* shows the direct influence of the great Classical epics; in any case it contains such features associated with the epic genre as the involvement of deities in the affairs of the heroes (Cú Chulainn is first harassed, then helped, by the war goddess Mórrigu and has the support of the sun god Lugh, treated in some versions as his real father), the lengthy cataloguing of forces involved, the conference of military leaders, and of course the full-scale battle. All O'Grady had to do, therefore, was to add some traditional stylistic devices, notably an invocation to the Muses and several heroic similes. His Gaelicized invocation was addressed to "spirits of the ancient bards, my ancestors, and ye sacred influences that haunt for ever the soil and air of my country, nameless now and unworshipped, but strong and eternal," and asked them to "be with me and befriend, that in circles worthy so glorious singing their praise upon whom nations looked back as upon their first and best, with a flight unfailing I may rise to regions where no wing of laborious ollav or chanting shanachie ever yet fanned that thinner air." The Miltonic seriousness with which O'Grady viewed his task was to be justified by the role his book came to play in reviving the worship of these "sacred influences," of modern Ireland's ancient heritage. There are heroic similes scattered throughout both volumes but they are not numerous enough to produce a strongly felt pattern. Only one of them is really memorable, and that because it involves another of those peculiar lapses of artistic taste to which O'Grady was subject: in it Cú Chulainn's chariot is compared to a fire apparatus: "and so drove Laeg, as when in a city in the night there is a cry of fire, and straightway with the sound of the horn, and thunder of wheels, and steel-shod hoofs, the rushing steeds bear onward through the dark streets the fire-subduers, and sparks fly out on every side from the smitten flint."

In the introduction to Volume One of the *History* O'Grady claimed to have used "the actual language of the bards, and as much as possible their style and

general character of expression." Such a medium would
have been appropriate indeed for his new Irish epic:
he himself said in the Preface to the 1882 *Cuculain*
volume that "that style which partly as a substitute for
metre I have adopted, and partly in imitation of the
bards, would seem rather to relegate [the book] to that
species of composition which is termed epic, than to
any other of the known kinds of literary workmanship."
Unfortunately no such medium existed. There was no
uniform "bardic" style: the surviving texts of the old
stories show tremendous variations in texture and or-
nateness, from the extremely simple and plain to the
wildest excesses and obscurities. O'Grady in practice
recognized this, for his medium is really an almost
purely conventional modern English, revealing as the
main stylistic influence upon it the prose of Carlyle.
Yeats has written perceptively about the difficulties
faced by O'Grady and other Irish writers in finding an
"answerable style": the only "Irish" form of English
available in the nineteenth century was the dialect used
by the novelists, and the unusual pronunciations in it
and its association with the "stage-Irish" stereotype had
given it indelible comic associations. It was not until
the next century that Lady Gregory and John Synge
each developed "Irish" styles in which there was no
attempt to indicate pronunciation, the Celtic flavor
coming from the use of syntax characteristic of that
English spoken by peasants in the West of Ireland
whose minds were still full of Irish constructions and
idioms. For Yeats this was the answer, and he considered the use of such a medium by Lady Gregory in her

own renderings of the Irish legends, *Cuchulain of Muir-themne* (1902) and *Gods and Fighting Men* (1904) a complete success. O'Grady himself was possibly less enthusiastic, for in a periodical he was editing he quoted at length a review of the earlier of the two in which T. W. Rolleston called her use of it an "unfortunate experiment" which he hoped she would not repeat.

In the areas of narrative organization and the depiction of characters, O'Grady made numerous and varied changes in his source material. His personal interests and biases provided the motives for many of these changes, while many others were of course necessitated by the unsatisfactory condition of the surviving texts: as O'Grady himself explained, in order "to be faithful to the generic conception, one must disregard often the literal statement of the bard. That the whole should be fairly represented, one must do violence to the parts, upon which, indeed, no more violence can be wrought than they inflict upon one another, perpetually diverging in detail, though in unison generally as to the main idea of characters and events." In other words, his first task was to eliminate contradictions and select from among variant accounts those which would be the most genuine, the closest to the "main idea." Here the requirement of faithfulness to the old stories presented no difficulties, as the process was simply one of separating what he considered to be the legitimate from the bogus and omitting the latter. His modifications, however, were not merely selective: he also took the far greater liberty of adding materials, either taken from other contexts or fabricated by himself. As an example of the former type, his impulse to tell *all* the stories, though it found fuller expression in later volumes, manifested itself in the *History* in the form of interpolated brief accounts of stories about several of the Tuatha Dé Danann and some incidents involving Red Branch figures but not relating closely to the Cattle Drive. Here, too, he could plausibly claim faithfulness to the "spirit" of the received documents. It was in the case of such inventions as the childhood scenes and the visit to Dublin that his position in this regard was weakest; for modern tastes at least, such breaches could not even be defended as improving the story *qua* story.

The coherent narrative into which he wove those episodes he considered genuine and those which he interpolated or made up is similarly open to criticism on aesthetic grounds. Some of the changes he made were perhaps successful in their effect. He divided the climactic battle between the Ultonians and the forces of Queen Medb into a two-day affair, with the men of Ulster losing the first day and triumphing on the second with the help of Cú Chulainn, in order to heighten suspense and make Cú's contribution seem even greater. Similarly, during the period in which Cú had singlehandedly been defending his home province O'Grady made his plight seem more terrible by depriving him of the comfort and aid even of Laeg, whom he has arrive only after the climactic combat with Fer Diad. On the other hand, among O'Grady's other additions was a series of incidents involving petty quarreling

between Medb and various other characters. These
incidents together receive a far greater amount of attention than their importance justifies, and have the distinctly negative effect of keeping Cú Chulainn "off
stage" for such long periods that he seems at times
almost forgotten. In other words, they dilute the inten-
sity of the narrative. And his handling of the Fer Diad
episode was particularly disappointing. O'Grady considered this scene the noblest episode in literature, and
while there are probably few who would place it quite
that high, it is certainly one of the most memorable
and one of the most perfectly told episodes in the
entire canon of early Irish literature, but O'Grady
rendered it in such a way as to strip it of virtually all
its power. In the original version the battle is divided
into several days, becoming each day more intense. The
first two nights, after fiercely combatting each other for
hours, the two heroes each

> went toward the other in the middle of the ford, and each
> of them put his hand on the other's neck and gave him
> three kisses in remembrance of his fellowship and friend-
> ship. Their horses were in one and the same paddock. . . ,
> and their charioteers at one and the same fire; and their
> charioteers made ready a litter-bed of fresh rushes for
> them with pillows for wounded men on them. Then came
> healing and curing folk to heal and to cure them, and
> they laid healing herbs and grasses and a curing charm
> on their cuts and stabs, their gashes and many wounds.
> Of every healing herb and grass and curing charm that
> was brought from the fairy dwellings of Erin to Cuchulain
> and was applied to the cuts and stabs, to the gashes and
> many wounds of Cuchulain, a like portion thereof he sent
> across the ford westward to Ferdiad

and "of every food and of every savoury, soothing and strong drink that was brought by the men of Erin to Ferdiad, a like portion thereof he sent over the ford northwards to Cuchulain. . . ." On the third day the combat is fiercer and less friendly, and the parting between them on the eve of what both know will be the decisive battle is a grim one: "they parted without a kiss, a blessing or aught other sign of friendship, and their servants disarmed the steeds, the squires and the heroes; no healing or curing herbs were sent from Cuchulain to Ferdiad that night, and no food nor drink was brought from Ferdiad to him. Their horses were not in the same paddock that night. Their charioteers were not at the same fire." Because the two are so evenly matched and because, being blood-brothers and boyhood friends, they are so reluctant to fight each other, the effect of the gradated divisions of the conflict is to heighten tremendously the suspense and emotional tension created by the story. For some reason O'Grady, though not at all afraid of diffuseness elsewhere, opted here for spareness and swiftness. Four days of combat are telescoped into one and the great battle is over in little more than a page. As such it scarcely stands out from the dozens of other individual duels in the "Cattle Drive," and O'Grady's enthusiasm for it could only puzzle the reader unfamiliar with its fuller form. In addition, O'Grady reduced to a single short paragraph the several pages of action which in the source follow Cú Chulainn's fatal casting of the *ga bulga,* though the material in question was of a type that usually appealed to him: the sentimental but noble lamentations of Cú

over the death of his friend. Perhaps for the moment
he felt simplicity to be preferable to sentiment, but in
view of the extreme fullness with which he had related
Fer Diad's original reluctance to take Medb's bribe to
fight Cú Chulainn and Cú's initial refusal to recognize
the challenge, the brevity of their final farewell makes
it seem inconsistent and highly anticlimactic.

Characterization in the modern sense may very well
have been a concern unknown to the makers of the
early Irish literature, but it was certainly a central one
of O'Grady's. He not only felt free to provide personali-
ties for many minor figures who were in the sources
almost uncharacterized, but also undertook major revisions in the treatment of the central characters. Of
course Cú Chulainn himself is the prime example, and
enough has already been said to make clear the extent
to which O'Grady remade his image. Fergus, Laeg, Fer
Diad, and Medb are among the others who received
close attention. The treatment of Medb was perhaps
most at variance with the source materials. O'Grady
tried to make her seem more "feminine," to endow her
with some of the personality traits traditionally associated with the "weaker sex," and at times the proud
amazon of the sources seems more like the delicate
fainting heroines of the nineteenth-century novel.

Thus O'Grady's method of turning the old texts into
"good stories" was not without serious flaws. But despite those flaws the *History* still "works," the intrinsic
virtues of the legends and O'Grady's strong enthusiasm
for them often compensating for failures in the rendering (there are, too, some notable successes), and—

particularly if the scarceness and generally poor quality of other literary treatments of the legendary materials available at the time is considered—it is easy to see how the book could have been so powerful in its impact upon those who read it.

Those who read it were, however, very few indeed and (although the book did receive some favorable reviews in the English press) O'Grady was discouraged. Then he had an experience, reminiscent of his discovery of O'Halloran's *History of Ireland,* which showed him a new course of action. Browsing one day in the library of the University Club he discovered that the club's copy of George Petrie's seminal archaeological study of the round towers of Ireland was uncut; this experience, his son relates, "opened his eyes to the mistake he had made. The public were not attracted by a sober treatise. Fiction and romance were their intellectual delicacies. Accordingly . . . he rewrote the Celtic legends in the guise of a novel." O'Grady's first attempts were not exactly "sober treatises," but clearly neither the "History" nor the "Epic" rubric would attract the great audience there was for fiction; and so he set to work upon what was to become a trilogy upon the life of Cú Chulainn. The first volume, *The Coming of Cuculain,* appeared in 1894; the second, *In the Gates of the North,* in 1901; and the third, *The Triumph and Passing of Cuculain,* not until 1920. The extended gaps in publication may have been partially the result of labors on other volumes and involvement in non-literary activities; but it is also a gauge of the fact that the trilogy, while drawing heavily upon its predecessor and preserving all the "epic" features except the invocation, was no mere reprint in disguise but a genuinely new work.

The Coming of Cuculain and In the Gates of the North covered Cú Chulainn's life to the same point as Volume One of the History, while The Triumph and Passing of Cuculain rehandled the material originally related in Volume Two. The Coming of Cuculain required by far the greatest revisions, for in the History O'Grady had dealt only very briefly with Cú's boyhood. In the new version (which he prefaced with a request that the reader "forget for a while that there is such a thing as scientific history" and "give his imagination a holiday") he had to go back and give substance to the outline of the events of Cú's early life as he had originally described them. Thus the action of the day upon which Cú took arms, which occupied eight pages in the History, is given nearly seventy in The Coming of Cuculain. In making this expansion, O'Grady continued to take the liberty he had originally allowed himself of inventing copious quantities of details—always, presumably, in the spirit of the original sources. And there was also a thorough revision of the verbal texture of the narrative.

Some idea of the various types of changes O'Grady made can be seen by comparing his two versions of a specific incident, the scene in which the young Cú (still called by his original name, Setanta) comes to Emain Macha, the capital city of the Red Branch, and sees there the young boy-warriors engaged in a game of hurley. He enters the game, not realizing that it is a

taboo for anyone to do so without first putting himself
under the protection of the group, and is attacked by
the others. He parries their assaults and then puts them
to flight, interrupting a chess game between Conchubor
and Fergus, who are impressed by him and make peace
in the group. The version given in the *History* stayed
fairly close to the source account, the main divergences
being the omission of some details about the weapons
cast at Cú and of a passage describing one of his "distortions." He also introduced a few things of his own,
such as the statement that the fleeing boys believed
their antagonist to be "one of the Tuatha from the
Fairy Hills of the Boyne"—a detail not in the sources
but plausible psychologically and in harmony with
O'Grady's desire to keep the entire panorama of ancient
legends before the reader. In *The Coming of Cuculain*
the episode is expanded enormously. The first new
change O'Grady made was the introduction of a "psy-
chological" passage describing Cú's feelings of grief and
disappointment when his arrival in Emain Macha is
ignored. Then he dramatized the initial conflict between him and the other boys and added such fabrica-
tions as having Cú identify himself to the boys as
Conchobor's nephew and the boys attack him because
they think he is lying. Next he invented an incident
depicting the Red Branch hero Conall Carnach starting
to intervene and then refraining when he "became
aware that this tumult was divinely guided." Following
that he brought in Laeg (whom in the sources and in
the *History* Cú meets at another time), having him take
Cú's part against the others as the battle resumes. In

addition to his need to lengthen the narrative, O'Grady's motivation here was obviously to heighten the dramatic effect of the episode and place emphasis from the first upon the strength of the friendship between Cú and Laeg. At the same time O'Grady was introducing all these new elements he eliminated some of those which in the *History* he had added to the received account, among them the reference to the Tuatha Dé Danann. And in one case, at least, he returned to the sources and adhered to them more closely than he had in the earlier version, putting in a brief and non-descriptive reference to the "distortion."

Even where the two versions remained close in regard to the action related, there were numerous verbal changes. In the *History* Cú's intrusion into the chess game was described as follows:

> The boy, however, running straight, sprang over the chess-table; but Concobar deftly seized him by the wrist, and brought him to a stand, but with dilated eyes, and panting.
>
> "Why are you so enraged, my boy?" said the king, "and why do you so maltreat my nobles?"
>
> "Because they have not treated me with the respect due to a stranger," replied the boy.
>
> "Who are you yourself?" said Concobar.
>
> "I am Setanta, the son of Sualtam, and Dectera, your own sister, is my mother; and it is not before my uncle's palace that I should be insulted and dishonored."

O'Grady then interjects the observation that "this was the debût and first martial exploit of the great Cuculain, type of Irish chivalry and courage, in the bardic firmament a bright particular star of strength, daring, and glory, that will not set or suffer aught but transient obscuration till the extinction of the Irish race. . . ." The narrative concludes with the information that "after this, Setanta was regularly received into the military school. . . . He placed himself under the tuition of Fergus MacRoy. . . ." This was the corresponding passage in *The Coming of Cuculain:*

> . . . Setanta running straight sprang lightly over the chess table. Then Conchobar, reaching forth his left hand, caught him by the wrist and brought him to a stand, panting and with dilated eyes.
>
> "Why art thou so enraged?" said the King, "and why dost thou so maltreat my boys?"
>
> It was a long time before the boy answered, so furiously burned the battle-fire within him, so that the King repeated his question more than once. At last he made answer—
>
> "Because they have not treated me with the respect due to a stranger."
>
> "Who art thou thyself?" said the King.
>
> "I am Setanta, son of Sualtam and of Dectera thy own sister, and it is not before my uncle's palace that I should be dishonoured."
>
> Conchobar smiled, for he was well pleased with the appearance and behavior of the boy, but Fergus caught him up in his great arms and kissed him, and he said—
>
> "Dost thou know me, O Setanta?"
>
> "I think thou art Fergus MacRoy," he answered.
>
> "Wilt thou have me for thy tutor?" said Fergus.
>
> "Right gladly," answered Setanta. "For in that hope too I left Dun Dalgan, coming hither secretly without the knowledge of my parents."
>
> This was the first martial exploit of Setanta.

In the revision O'Grady changed the form of address used from "you" to "thou" forms, and added some specific details, such as "*left* hand." In the *History* he

had repeatedly used "but" where "and" and other con-
nectives would more normally be used; throughout the
trilogy he virtually eliminated this usage, as here in
the cases of "but Conchobar deftly seized him . . ."
and "but with dilated eyes. . . ." (In the case of "but
Fergus caught him up . . ." O'Grady presumably did
intend to convey contrast.) Even so slight a matter as
the rather confusing use in the *History* of "nobles" for
"boys" is corrected. In the *History* there were passages,
such as the one quoted above in which Cú's heroism is
praised, in which the narrative was interrupted by the
voice of O'Grady as "historian"; but the more uni-
formly "literary" texture of the new version made such
passages stand out too awkwardly. Such was apparently
the reason for the omission of the paragraph in question
here. One further noteworthy change is the effort to
achieve greater immediacy by dramatizing the choosing
of Fergus as Cú's tutor and relating it through direct
discourse.

In the Gates of the North (which O'Grady, with one
last, feeble glance in the direction of his "archaeological" concerns, called an "heroic, romantic, and semi-
historic Irish tale") and *The Triumph and Passing of
Cuculain* required no such large-scale addition of
materials as had *The Coming of Cuculain*. However,
in addition to continuing to adjust the texture of the
work, O'Grady did make several changes in the narrative, even omitting some whole scenes while adding
others.

In general the trilogy, though thoroughly rewritten,
has the same basic shape as its earlier form, and is not

noticeably *better* from an aesthetic point of view. However, it probably would still have achieved something
of the greater circulation for which O'Grady had hoped
if its publication had not been so long a process. The
first volume, brought out over the prestigious name of
Methuen, was well received and enthusiastically propagandized for by Yeats; unfortunately *In the Gates of
the North* did not appear for seven years, and then
without the benefit of a publisher who could give it
wide distribution. And it was not until about twenty
years later that the Talbot Press made all three volumes
available in a uniform format. By that time other, more
polished treatments of the old legends were available,
including Lady Gregory's two volumes, and the
legendary materials no longer possessed the novelty
they had had when O'Grady had begun his task. As a
result it was primarily the *History,* scarce as it was and
full of false starts and hesitations in method, through
which his vision of Ireland's heroic past made its
impact upon the modern Irish consciousness.

Between the appearance of the *History* and the first
volume of the Cú Chulainn trilogy O'Grady published
one other literary rendering of the early Irish legendary
materials, *Finn and His Companions* (1892). The
legends of the "Fenian Cycle," though even more frag-
mented than the Red Branch stories as they have come
down to us, provide a similar opportunity for con-
structing a coherent narrative. Such a narrative, arranged chronologically, would begin with Fionn's
father, Cumhall. In the Battle of Cnucha he was slain
by Goll macMorna, who thus gained control of the

Fianna and tried to protect his position by having all of Cumhall's family and supporters killed. But Fionn (an infant at the time) was saved, and when he reached manhood he won back his father's place. Following this in the narrative would come a long series of incidents concerning notable events which occurred while Fionn was captain of the Fianna, the most famous of those events being unquestionably the story of Diarmaid and Gráinne. Finally Fionn's power declined, especially after the Battle of Gabhra, and the Fianna faded away. However, at least one member of the group—Fionn's son Oisin in one version and the warrior Caoilte in another—was traditionally depicted as having survived until the time of Saint Patrick and having communicated to him the history of Fionn and his men.

In contrast to his approach in the *History,* O'Grady did not in *Finn and His Companions* attempt to re-create this entire narrative. Perhaps he lacked sufficient time or felt that such treatment would be inappropriate for these materials. In addition, the book was published in Fisher Unwin's "Children's Library" series, and the youthful potential audience meant that any incidents involving sex or showing the main characters in an unfavorable light would have to be cut out. Of course O'Grady had made similar omissions in the *History,* but here the effect was more damaging to the total impact of the book, for it meant sacrificing the crown jewel of the cycle, the Diarmaid and Gráinne episode. That episode was not only full of desire and passion, but even worse, it depicted Gráinne as being unfaithful to the memory of Diarmaid and Fionn as breaking his word to the lovers and then refusing to save the dying Diarmaid when he easily could have done so. On the other hand, those episodes O'Grady did use seem to have been chosen primarily for moralistic reasons rather than with aesthetic excellence in mind. He began his volume with the encounter of Caoilte and Patrick; this was morally acceptable, for O'Grady made an angel appear to Patrick and reveal to him that Fionn was a "prophet without full knowledge" who "had prepared the minds of the Gael for the preaching of Christ's gospel." Inexplicably, however, he did not use the natural device of having *Caoilte* then narrate the stories that follow. The result is of course a sense of disjointedness. And in the arrangement of those stories the moral scheme is again clear, the artistic blurred. Several incidents involving Fionn's generosity are followed by Fionn's own account to a "historian" of some events from his childhood, and then by the story of his revelation of himself to the small band of Fianna who had remained loyal to the memory of his father and of how he regained his father's position. "The lesson taught by Finn in his power," O'Grady informs his readers, "is the lesson of flowing goodwill towards men. From his youth we learn the lesson of cheerfulness and courage." Unfortunately, the highly selective and chronologically confusing narrative which results from the arrangement of the episodes in this pattern has little literary appeal and might be difficult even to follow for those having only slight familiarity with the traditional legends.

In view of these weaknesses, it might seem surprising

to find Yeats—usually highly judicious in his evalua-
tions of Irish literature—calling *Finn and His Companions* "wonderful and incomparable" and O'Grady's
"masterpiece." These estimates do in fact seem excessive, but it is also clear from the specific elements to
which he responded that his attitude *was* an intelligent
and sensitive one. He liked the vividness of O'Grady's
picture of the "Ossianic age," and termed the language
of the book (which was simpler and less turgid than
the medium he had employed in the *History*) "both
powerful and beautiful." Most importantly, the episode
that made the strongest impression upon him was the
finest part of the volume by literary standards—that
dealing with Fionn's encounter with the old men whose
loyalty to his father had forced them to lead a life of
isolation, danger, even near starvation in the midst
of their enemies. This episode had been in O'Grady's
mind at least as early as 1881, for in a footnote in the
History of Ireland: Critical and Philosophical he had
spoken of the brief source passage as material for a
"noble scene." In his own rendering of it he made full
use of the "good story" method, expanding it greatly
and adding not only copious details but also a full
exploration of the emotional content only implicit in
the original. Three years after reading the book Yeats
referred to this section and quoted from it a phrase
describing the old men's bewilderment at the tears
Fionn sheds upon discovering their pathetic situation:
"Youth, they thought, hath many sorrows which old age
cannot comprehend." Obviously part of the appeal here
was personal, for Yeats himself was at this time—1895—

experiencing both economic hardship and the pains of frustrated love, but the passage is powerful even for those who do not find in it an objective correlative; AE later singled out the same sentence for praise. But the most dramatic testimony of how strongly Yeats was affected by the scene is found in the fact that it reappeared in his work almost half a century later, when he wrote what was to be his last poem, "The Black Tower": the warriors' dire prospects, the strength of their allegiance, and their faith that their leader's faction would again triumph all supported Yeats's allegorical depiction of himself as dying in an alien world but still faithful to those ideals he had held and confident that the whirling of the gyres would eventually bring them to prominence once more.

2.
O'Grady and Tudor Ireland

In 1881 O'Grady published the first volume of what
was intended to be a *comprehensive* history of Ireland,
the book already referred to as the *History of Ireland:
Critical and Philosophical.* No further volumes ever
appeared, perhaps because the first had caused little
stir, perhaps because the job was bigger than he had
anticipated. (Many years later he did do a *very* brief
sketch of the subject called *The Story of Ireland.*)
Nevertheless, he did read extensively in the periods of
Irish history that followed the ancient culture on which
he had originally focused. One period in particular
fascinated him, and it held him until he had made
himself expert in its lore and written a number of
books dealing with it: this was the sixteenth-century
Ireland of the Tudors. The century marked a major
watershed in Irish history. At the beginning of it
England in practice controlled only a small portion of
the country, the area known as "the Pale"; the rest was
in the hands of various often hostile native chieftains

and Gaelicized Anglo-Normans. By 1603 the entire
country had been brought under control and virtually
all resistance to English domination crushed.

What was the source of the fascination which it held
for O'Grady? The answer can be found in this description of the era by the modern historian Edmund
Curtis: "the old Gaelic world, which had existed for
two thousand years, was now to clash with the modern
world as represented by the Tudor government. . . .
[The Gaelic world's] ideal was that of an aristocracy
who still lived in the Irish heroic age, in the atmosphere
of battle and foray. . . ." In other words, O'Grady saw
here the last stand of that culture whose greatness in
primitive ages had generated his first interest in his
own country and had been the subject of his early
writings.

He saw, furthermore, a number of specific parallels
between the two epochs. As the seat of the Red Branch
heroes who dominated the most noble of the epic cycles
had been in what is now Ulster, so the Irish lords who
led the resistance to the triumph of English rule were
primarily from the same northern province. Foremost
among these were Hugh O'Neill, Earl of Tyrone, and
Red Hugh O'Donnell. In contrast to his treatment of
the heroic period, O'Grady by no means idealized the
Irish Tudor era: he in fact stressed at length its seamy
underside, with nearly everyone in *both* groups willing
to engage in such practices as bribery, betrayal, and
even assassination, "the dagger and the bowl." But
from his almost blanket condemnation he excepted
both O'Neill and the "brave and chivalrous" O'Don-

nell, who especially attracted him and who because of his youth and courage seemed to be almost a new Cú Chulainn. O'Grady drew these parallels overtly in a passage in one of his books on Red Hugh, *The Flight of the Eagle*: "his bardic eulogizers have compared Hugh Roe to the antique hero Cuculain, son of Sualtam. Hugh was just now riding through the chief theatre of Cuculain's exploits, past Ardee, the Ford of Far-dia, where he stood, as it were, in the gap of Ulster, and held the gates of the province against Queen Maeve's host, past dolmen and mound marking the graves of champions whom he had slain." He went on to suggest that the earlier hero was actually part of the consciousness of the later one: "Hugh talked with Turlough [his guide] on that theme as they rode through these classic plains, for to every well-nurtured lad of the free nations of Ireland all those sublime beings of the dim dawn were very real and alive." And this passage is followed closely by a chapter called "Through the Mountain Gates of Ulster"—a chapter which moved Yeats deeply and stayed with him for a long time—in which not the mere Red Branch Cycle but rather all of "Gaelic tradition" is brought to bear upon the career of Hugh. The occasion of the chapter is Hugh's passing of the mountain Slieve Gullion, which O'Grady treats as a sort of "holy mountain" of Ireland, linked with Cú Chulainn (who found there his fabulous horse the Liath Macha), Fionn, the gods, the sacred hazel tree and "the well of the waters of all wisdom." Of the "mythus" it represents, Hugh was "the last great secular champion." O'Grady saw the defeat of Hugh and his allies as necessary for Ireland to pass from barbarism to civilization, but the larger significance which the event held in his eyes made it seem at the same time "profoundly tragic."

This crucial period, like the ancient heroic age, seemed to O'Grady to be less well known and understood than it ought to be, and he tried here too to remedy the situation personally. Predictably, the works he produced on the subject reveal the same vacillation between the scholarly and the imaginative which characterized the *History* and its successors. At one extreme was his edition of *Pacata Hibernia* (1896), a contemporary account of part of the "Nine Years' War" in which the Gaelic chieftains were finally overcome; at the other was his little play *Hugh Roe O'Donnell* (1902). In between these volumes fall several other books, notably *Red Hugh's Captivity* (1889); a revision of this book called *The Flight of the Eagle* (1897); a collection of short stories, *The Bog of Stars* (1893); and the historical novel *Ulrick the Ready* (1896).

Introductory statements in both *Red Hugh's Captivity* and *The Flight of the Eagle* show O'Grady struggling for a definition of his approach that would appease both of his conflicting impulses. In the former his declaration that "I would bring before the mind, as vividly as I can, and also as truthfully and historically as I can, the actualities of the times . . ." imposes a rhetorical balance that mutes potential opposition. A few pages later he put the nature of the period itself to similar use, asserting that in it "the actualities of history become themselves a romance. The facts, well told, ought to surpass fiction, even in those respects in which fiction is most delightful. The historian relating only what is recorded may supply pictures of scenes and events, and portraits of historic figures, which in moving interest ought to bear comparison with the best imaginative work." Although the book in its rewritten form had the more glamorous title *The Flight of the Eagle,* the approach taken towards the material was essentially the same as in *Red Hugh's Captivity,* and in the Preface to the later book O'Grady was at pains to make it clear that "this tale, in spite of its title, is not a romance, but an actual historic episode, told with hardly a freer use of the historical imagination than is employed by the more popular and picturesque of our professed historians." Then, immediately shifting in the opposite direction, he made the important qualification that "there is, however, this difference between my method and theirs, viz. that while they write directly I aim at a similar result through a certain dramatization. The same method has been adopted, I think very effectively, by Carlyle, at times, in his history of Frederick the Great." The term "dramatization" is actually rather misleading: the story is really much more narrated than dramatized, the author's voice is dominant throughout and there are virtually no "scenes" in which individuals come together and engage in dialogue. In practice the technique involved narration heavily charged with graphic descriptions and punctuated frequently with analytic passages.

The subject with which O'Grady was working was

an intrinsically exciting one and required little "improvement" to give it the appeal of romance. At the time of the Armada scare the English viceroy in Ireland, Sir John Perrott, sought hostages from all the important Irish families in order to insure that they would not attempt an alliance with Spain. When the O'Donnells refused to send in a hostage, Perrott resorted to deception: he concealed a troop of soldiers aboard a ship and sent it to the O'Donnells' country, ostensibly to trade in wines; young Hugh, lured on board, was captured and taken to Dublin, where he was imprisoned in Dublin Castle. His first escape effort failed when he took refuge at the home of a man who delivered him back to the English. A second flight proved successful, though he was permanently lamed by prolonged exposure in the snowy countryside. Rather than having to shape his material aesthetically and morally, delete offensive elements and fabricate others, O'Grady's main task was to develop the circumstantiality of the facts, to bring them "vividly" before the mind. In order to achieve "the colouring, the visualization and dramatization," he drew not only upon the historical documents dealing with Hugh, but also upon "a wider circle of contemporary literature." And as in the *History* he had felt free to intersperse the epic adventures with descriptions of various aspects of ancient Irish society, so in these volumes he tried "to interweave the contemporary history of Ireland, and reflect the temper and manners of the age."

While there was no real shift in approach between *Red Hugh's Captivity* and *The Flight of the Eagle,*

O'Grady did make some significant revisions. The earlier book contained numerous footnotes, mainly referring to scholarly sources; in *The Flight of the Eagle* these were relegated to an appendix. A few changes of fact were made, some irrelevant materials pruned away, and the progress of the narrative made smoother in a number of places. Most important of all, however, was a shift in emphasis from "captivity" to "flight." In the revised version Hugh's successful escape, which had been treated rather abruptly in the early volume, is given greatly extended treatment. Among the new materials were both the comparison of Hugh to Cú Chulainn and the entire "Through the Mountain Gates of Ulster" chapter.

The prose style of both versions is generally similar, and while lucid and graphic, not very striking. The one exception is the "Slieve Gullion" passage in "Through the Mountain Gates of Ulster," which becomes increasingly lyrical and effusive as it reaches its climax in an address to the fabled Lough Liath, the Grey Lake, supposed to be found at its peak:

O melancholy lake, shaped like the moon! lake uplifted high in the arms of Slieve Gullion; boggy, desolate, thick-strewn with grey boulders on thy eastern shore and, on thy western, regarded askance by thy step-child the rosy heather, ruddy as with blood—aloof, observant of thy never-ending sorrow; unfathomable, druid lake: home of the white steed immortal: bath of the Caillia-Bullia, the people's dread; thy turbid waves aye breaking in pale foam upon thy grey shore strewn with boulders and the wrecks of the work of men's hands; horror-haunted, enchanted lake; seat of dim ethnic mysteries, lost all or scattered to the winds; with thy made wells and walls and

painted temples and shining cairns, and subterrene corri-
dors obscure—walked once by druids gold-helmeted and
girded with the Sun;—scene of religious pomps, and
thronging congregations hymning loud their forgotten
gods obscene or fair; what mighty tales, what thoughts
far-journeying, Protean, sprang once in light from thy
wine-dark, mystic floor, Lough Liath! Sky-neighbouring
lake vexed by all the winds! mournful, sibilant, teeming
fount of thy vast phantasmal mythus, O Ultonia!

The passage ends with a reflection upon the ultimate
failure of Hugh's struggle, the result of "the weaving
stars." The very rhythms of the prose (especially in
such phrases as "thy turbid waves aye breaking in pale
foam upon thy grey shore strewn with boulders and
the wrecks of the work of men's hands") as well as
the sense of doomed bravery, the misty, vaguely "spiritual" atmosphere perfectly exemplify the "Celtic twi-
light" mode that colored Irish literature during the
middle and late 1890s, and it is no surprise that Yeats
singled out this passage for special praise in his contemporary review of the book.

O'Grady's final reworking of the story of Red Hugh's
captivity and escape was his play *Hugh Roe O'Donnell.*
More a dramatization of a series of scenes than a genuine drama, this work was actually performed by a group
of amateurs in 1902. O'Grady himself took a minor
role. But if the play itself is very slight, it is clear
nevertheless that O'Grady took it seriously, even including certain incidents that he had not treated in
his earlier works on the subject. The most interesting
element in the play is a further reference to Cú Chulainn: the lyrical passages from *The Flight of the Eagle*

had to be omitted, but as Hugh rides past Slieve Gullion he declares that "my benefactor—the spirit of Cuchullin—broods over it this night—I feel stronger as the bracing air through the Gates of the North strikes my brow." This was the fullest identification O'Grady made between his two ideal heroes.

Red Hugh, at a later stage in his career, also appeared in one of the sketches in *The Bog of Stars and Other Stories of Elizabethan Ireland* (1893). The brief prefatory note to this volume revealed the familiar O'Grady ambiguity concerning the nature of his work: "the following stories are not so much founded on fact as in fact true. The events are in each case related either as they actually occurred or with a very slight dramatization and infusion of local and contemporaneous colour. My object generally has been to bring the modern Irish reader into closer and more sympathetic relation with a most remarkable century of Irish history; one which, more than any other, seems to have determined the destiny of Ireland." The book contains nine stories, with no narrative continuity or chronological arrangement, and among them there is considerable variation in the extent of "literary" treatment. Some of them hardly deserve to be called "stories" at all, being mere biographical accounts with no "plot" or "dramatization"; others are fully dramatized and have a more extensive use of dialogue than either *Red Hugh's Captivity* or *The Flight of the Eagle*. The entire collection is virtually free of the copious analytic passages which characterize both of those books. In general the volume is not a particularly memorable one, but the title story, dealing with a young drummer-boy who gave his life in order to warn an Irish chief of an impending attack on his stronghold, shows as much artistry as almost anything O'Grady ever wrote. His manipulation of tone and image in the passage describing the execution of the boy is particularly note-worthy.

The Bog of Stars was probably the only one of his books to obtain anything approaching a popular audi-ence. It was published as part of the New Irish Library, a project conceived by Yeats and the old Young Ire-lander Charles Gavan Duffy as a means for getting good literature into the hands of the Irish masses. There was a serious difference of opinion between Yeats and Duffy concerning the kind of literature to include; the latter desired patriotic fragments of a past era while the former wanted the works of the best writers of his own time. O'Grady was of course one of Yeats's choices. Duffy gained effectual control of the project and soon destroyed its appeal by publishing works that satisfied his own preferences, but *The Bog of Stars* appeared early enough to profit from the widespread enthusiasm that had been aroused at first. Thus at least one of the Tudor volumes found an audience broader than that small group of imaginative writers and occasional mem-bers of the leisured classes who ordinarily read him.

Ulrick the Ready (1896) is really an historical novel, though O'Grady appeased his scholarly conscience with some footnotes, an appendix, and the protestation that "though the work is a romance, I know that the his-torical setting is in the main correct, and believe that the colouring and dramatization supply a true picture of the manners and men of the age. . . . It is not a story all in the air, but one rooted in fact." And in the text itself, as Boyd has suggested, O'Grady showed great competence in the assimilation of his storehouse of facts into the fabric of the story: "the manner in which he handles his historical material has lost all the clumsiness of his first effort at long narrative, the odour of the archives no longer hangs about his pages, and the ease and fluency of the story indicates a complete mastery of detail." The historical background involves the Battle of Kinsale in 1601, and Red Hugh makes yet another appearance, but the focus of the book is upon the character Ulrick, essentially a fictional creation. The characterization is very full and in general successful, but the later portions of the book are marred by the introduction of a highly sentimental love interest. There is far more dialogue than in any of the other Tudor volumes, and even some comedy. But even while indulging himself in such an approach O'Grady was keeping in mind his more "serious" concerns, not only in the introduction of Red Hugh but also through a series of epigraphs and allusions in the text to the legends of Cú Chulainn, Fionn, and other legendary figures.

In addition to the books dealing with this period of Irish history, O'Grady during his long career wrote a number of other pieces of fiction. These include *In the Wake of King James* (1896), a romance; *The Departure of Dermot* (first published 1901), a short sketch dealing with the events that led to the Norman occu-

pation of Ireland; two boys' tales, *Lost on Du-Corrig*
(1894) and *The Chain of Gold* (1895); and the uto-
pian fantasy *The Queen of the World* (1900), so
different from the rest of his work that he published
it pseudonymously. None of these added substantially
to his reputation or brought him great commercial
success, and in perspective they seem mere appendages
to the body of work dealing with the Irish sixteenth
century.

3.
O'Grady and Modern Ireland

O'Grady's antiquarian and literary pursuits did not keep him from being interested in what was happening in Ireland in his own day; on the contrary, they helped turn his attention in that direction and even to a great extent shaped his personal vision of contemporary problems. For him, as for so many of his countrymen, the present moment was haunted by awareness of the past.

O'Grady came from a family of gentlemen and small landowners, and grew up with an aristocratic bias and a dislike for democracy. Not even Whitman, whose early and enthusiastic admirer O'Grady was, could make what he considered "mob rule" acceptable to him. When he began to immerse himself in the early legend and history of Ireland it gave him more of an interest in his own land than was to be found in most members of the Ascendancy, but it also made him think of that class in even grander terms. O'Grady viewed the Irish past as a "prophecy of the future." He believed that "the gigantic conceptions of heroism and strength, with which the forefront of Irish history is thronged, prove the great future of this race and land." As his mind became saturated with images of Cú Chulainn and the other leaders of Ireland in ages past, those images led him to conceive a similarly noble and heroic role for the "ruling" class of his own time. As E. A. Boyd put it, "there is no doubt that the author of the Bardic History owed his belief in the destiny of the Irish aristocracy to the contageous grandeur of the narratives of that ancient order which he had evoked with the intuitive sympathy of genius." They were the heirs of that order and the destined inheritors of its virtues, and it was their job to affect the course of modern Ireland with those virtues. They might especially exert a social and cultural influence upon the popular forces which O'Grady feared were certain to become increasingly powerful: they should

> be felt and known to be, the highest moral element, the light, the ornament, and the conscience of the young barbaric power now ascending in our land, of this fierce, dark, vengeful democracy, soon to be let loose with all its savage instincts uncontrolled . . . soothing the passage between caste and equality, softening, healing, consolidating, mitigating, preserving and transmitting to new generations the social ideal as this younger birth, trumpet-tongued, comes proclaiming the political—grace, courtesy, refinement, moderation and modesty, politeness, and its great parent kindness between man and man, sensibility and personal pride. . . .

Furthermore, the triumph of republicanism seemed likely to have as a concomitant the triumph of mammonism, and the landowners, emanating from "a class in which wealth and rank, long inherited and taken as matters of course are . . . slightly regarded," could act as a counter-force. In this conception of the Ascendancy he closely anticipated the position to which Yeats was to come in later years, when he would oppose "Paudeenism" with the rich tradition embodied in Coole Park and in the Anglo-Irish eighteenth century.

But the landlord class that O'Grady found about him in the late 'seventies and early 'eighties was far from coinciding with the noble image he had conceived for it, and furthermore was at a point of crisis which threatened its very existence. The Georgian period in Ireland (where Yeats would find his own aristocratic ideal) had been a time of great material prosperity and of brilliant cultural accomplishments for this class. But various political developments, especially the legislative union with England in 1800, changed all this. The country began to suffer financially and economically. More and more landlords became "absentees," seldom if ever residing in their own country and leaving their property to decline in real value while seeking to wring excessive rents from it; the natural result was growing agrarian unrest. And all these problems were compounded by the Great Famine of the late 'forties and land speculation in the 'fifties. In 1879, while O'Grady was in the process of bringing out his *History of Ireland,* Michael Davitt founded the Land League. The League, the purpose of which was to win fair rent practices and aid the passing of land ownership from the landlords to the tenants, attacked the current system at its base. O'Grady was appalled by what he felt to be the failure of the landlords to make any concerted effort to protect their position during this period of agitation, boycotting, and agrarian violence. Thus he began, as Yeats later characterized it, to "rage over their failings" and in a long series of works to sing their "swan song."

The *History of Ireland* itself showed the imprint of O'Grady's concern for the contemporary situation. A footnote in the 1880 volume observed that social conditions for the majority of people during the ancient period were better than in modern Ireland: "not only were the rents for the most part protected by law, but those rents were again spent in the country." A second direct reference was even more negative, for it suggested that while the landlords were ineffectual in defending their position they had at the same time become infected with the very mammonism which as he conceived their role it was their duty to oppose: in the text of the second volume he included the observation that "in the days of Maeve, the great knights and champions of Eiré concerned themselves with more knightly deeds and thoughts, and relinquished to the base-born excessive zeal concerning wealth and its distribution."

However, it was in the first volume, which had appeared even before the founding of the League, that O'Grady gave the most extended, if indirect, expression to his fears. Most of O'Grady's modifications of his sources were designed to improve them artistically or morally. But in one instance he fabricated an episode not to enhance the aesthetic virtues of the story or to bring it in line with his idealized image of the heroic age, or even to add another element to his portrait of social life in that age, but rather to create a fable for his own time. In doing so he was anticipating the approach of Yeats, who was to be the first writer to use the Irish legends as vehicles for self-expression—sources of allegory and symbol, "objective correlatives" for his own feelings and ideas. O'Grady himself, however, would have rejected the egotism in Yeats's approach; his own fable was an impersonal one and had "general betterment" as its purpose.

The incident in question occurs as Laeg, who in O'Grady's version has been separated from Cú Chulainn during most of the latter's battles against the forces of Medb, is rushing to rejoin his master. Tired, and with his chariot in need of repair, he seeks shelter for the night at the nearest house. To his surprise he finds men still working in the fields, though it is already dark. Approaching the owner of the estate he asks for hospitality and assistance, but to his amazement the owner, whose life Cú Chulainn had once saved, refuses. Originally an exile and a slave, he had gradually obtained some land of his own and avariciously accumulated considerable wealth. Because he did *not* come from a class in which wealth and rank, long inherited, were lightly weighed, he has a strictly selfish view of courtesy and hospitality: he tells Laeg that "it was not by the lavish entertainment of those who passed by this way that I have become rich and great as thou now see'st me, but by prudence and attention to my several affairs. If I supply thee and thine with entertainment and the labour of my slaves, look to it, I shall require a suitable reward!" He even pays lip-service to the "blessed Shee," praying and saving like Yeats's Paudeens in their shops. As Laeg sees, "romantic Ireland" will really be dead and gone if this sort of man is allowed to flourish unchecked: "an evil time, indeed, will it be for the Gaeil if the ollavs and their wisdom concur to plant among us such shrubs of deadly poison as thyself, O vile and avaricious stranger, without gratitude or nobleness or love for aught save thy miserable accumulation of sorry pelf." He then beats him and ties him up so he will have to look on helplessly as Laeg helps himself to the things that he needs. The "right" side wins here, but the tenor of the fable is clearly a warning to the upper classes of what would happen if they did not assert themselves: the passing of the land into the hands of men with no trace of the old heroic qualities.

This episode stands out dramatically in its context, and the veil of fable is quite thin. Nevertheless it is doubtful whether even if the *History* had been a commercial success and reached the audience O'Grady had had in mind, they would have been affected—those for whom such omens are intended usually being the last to recognize the application to themselves. In the future O'Grady generally would adopt much more direct methods of addressing that audience. Interestingly enough, however, he did revive the indirect method in *Finn and His Companions,* perhaps feeling that it might reach his youthful readers. He invented an incident in which Fionn and his men are coldly received by one Nod, whom they bind and force to watch as they make use of his jealously protected stores. Eventually they actually succeed in teaching him the error of his ways and he becomes a good man. Nod, O'Grady explains, represents "penury itself," and "the story shows how Finn by force, example, and precept, taught the men of Ireland to live in a more generous, kindly, and humane manner than they had done." This, of course, was the effect that O'Grady hoped the landlord class would have upon the "new" men of the country.

Only shortly after the appearance of the *History* O'Grady adopted a far more practical method for influencing the contemporary course of these affairs. In late 1881 he arranged a Landlords' Meeting in Dublin to consider the current situation, and a second meeting was held in 1882. In that same year he published the pamphlet *The Crisis in Ireland,* in which he expressed his personal appraisal of that situation. The landlords had done nothing concrete themselves, while a new Land Act had been passed which further weakened their position. O'Grady, assuming the role and voice of an Old Testament prophet, sought desperately to make them aware of their true plight. He himself had no solution to offer; he merely hoped that, once awakened, they would do *something,* and thus insure at least "the preservation of the Irish landlords as a class, though divested of territorial power." To this end he adopted a position of brutal frankness, accusing them of having failed to act during the first year of the Land League, when they might have been able to make reasonable settlements, and evoking the specters of growing world-wide socialism, mass violence, and the forcing of the gentry to desert their property entirely and seek military protection. In order to smash their illusion that England would help them, he created an imaginary dialogue between them and Gladstone, currently the Liberal Prime Minister, in which the latter, now that the Irish upper classes were no longer strong enough to be a valuable political ally, flatly rejects their pleas. He predicted apocalyptically that "only the utmost wisdom and circumspection, and the utmost courage, quickness, and determination, with the adoption of wholly new counsels, will avail to save from destruction a class, without them wholly and irretrievably doomed," but he was mindful of how at the time of the Union they had "sold to England the independence of their country and their own great future as the leaders of a nation, for a paltry sum of money, or for still paltrier baubles and trappings, and exchanged, for ignoble sloth and abject, uneventful lives, a career of high effort, beneficent activity, and glorious responsibility" (here clearly the image of the epic past was before his eyes) ; thus he had ultimately very little confidence that they *would* act now. And he was correct in lacking that confidence, for if they heard his message this time they neither understood it nor acted upon it. Boyd has described their surprise when, after having heartily agreed with his denunciations of their enemies, he went on to speak not of their own rights and privileges but rather of their duties; in fact, if they had been perceptive enough to understand him, they probably would not have fallen into such a predicament in the first place.

Thus they continued to remain inert while the movement grew which gradually—precisely as O'Grady had envisioned—did almost completely wipe them out.

O'Grady himself, however, was far from through with his personal fight. In 1882 he had had no specific practical plan to propose; four years later, in 1886, he did see such a plan, and presented it in published form under the title *Toryism and the Tory Democracy*. The traditional Tory Party in England and its Irish adherents were, he felt, out of touch with the facts of contemporary political life and doing far more harm than good. Against this traditional Toryism he set up the so-called "Tory Democracy" recently conceived by Lord Randolph Churchill. Lord Randolph saw that the populace had become a major force in modern life, and wanted the Conservatives to recognize this and make every effort to win the popular element for their own party. He hoped to involve the working classes in Tory Democracy and thus prevent a combination of capital and labor against the old landed aristocracy.

O'Grady's application of this principle to Ireland came in two parts. In the first, an address "to the Landlords of Ireland," he set out to destroy whatever illusions they might have left about their security and their future. Not only had they not done anything since the last time he had addressed them to avert the impending catastrophe, but they had even steered *towards* the precipice. He expressed the belief that there had never been "an aristocracy so rotten in its seeming strength, so recreant, resourceless, and stupid in the day of trial, so degenerate, outworn and effete," an "ease-

loving and unheroic race of Irish landlords." Occasion-
ally his scorn became so strong that he seems almost to
have lost control, producing such outbursts as "Christ
save us all! You read nothing, know nothing." He
frequently contrasted their present degraded condition
with the deeds of their early predecessors and in one
instance specifically referred to Red Hugh, character-
izing him as one who "would have offered but a short
shrift to a committee of modern patriots going down
to organize his tenantry on National League principles
—that same lame, tameless fighter and harryer of the
North-West." For them as a class he had now "not the
least hope," and he announced dramatically "you have
outlived your day." He did, however, continue to have
hope for at least some individuals, and the second part
of this "Ireland and the Hour" section was addressed
to one such hypothetical individual. Here he put forth
his specific scheme. First of all, the landlord was to get
on his estate and stay there, eschewing the temptation
of absenteeism. Then his main task was to invest his
wealth in *men,* hiring labor and employing it in industries on the estate. These men were to be not mere
employees but loyal retainers who loved and feared
him and whom he controlled with a gentle but very
firm hand. He might also have in his service, as over-
seers of the workers, displaced members of his own
class. This arrangement would have economic advan-
tages itself and also would help curb agrarian agitation
by making the interests of the workers opposed to rent-
withholding and similar tactics by the farmers. Several
times O'Grady revealed that the model he had in mind

for this new relationship was a feudal one, and again he found specifically Irish precedents. In one place he even directly suggested to his ideal individual that "there has been a great deal of wisdom as well as valour and goodness in this poor distressful country, and her history, when you, or men such as you, dig it out like gold from the depths of our manuscripts and printed archives, will prove, in a sense you can now little realize, veritably a light to your feet and a lamp to your path." In fact, during this section, which is a triumph of sustained rhetorical virtuosity, O'Grady became so convinced by his own proposal that at the end his tone became almost optimistic:

> Volunteers . . . of all kinds and types will flock towards you; youths brave and bold, high-spirited, of mettle and honour, gracious, too, and gentle, the man-ruling born captains of the world; youths with plotting, planning, deep-calculating brains, scientific or otherwise; tongues of fire, that can inflame men with their own burning zeal, tongues dropping words of wisdom in the secret ear; youths studious and literary (don't forget this one great task of the future Ireland's history) ; men and minds of many types and of all types, see that you make yourself fit to be their king. As sure as I write these words they will gather to you from the north, the south, the east, and the west, out of Ireland, and out of all lands.

This optimism was of course tragically unjustified. According to O'Grady's son, some few "distinguished landowners" were led by the book to attempt a revival of Irish industries and did build up labor forces on their own estates; but they had only a token effect, and for the class as a whole conditions continued to grow

worse. Ironically, the book itself has come to be thought
of as O'Grady's most successful attempt at political
writing, perceptive in its analysis of the changing nature
of modern economic and social structures and memorable in its impassioned prose.

O'Grady's vehement castigations of his own class soon
led others to believe that he had changed his political
orientation; in 1890 Yeats, who attributed his "political
vagaries" to a Carlylean "love of force," found it "pretty
plain that Mr. O'Grady is seeing the error of his ways
and growing into a good Nationalist after all." This
was not in fact correct: though for the time being
O'Grady was disillusioned with the group that he had
hoped would rule or at least guide the country, he still
felt that the place of Ireland was in the Empire.
Towards the end of the decade an event took place
which at least temporarily made him even more certain of the wisdom of that connection, while at the
same time promising a solution to the problem of the
failure of the landlords to assume what he considered
to be their natural position.

While O'Grady, in rewriting *Red Hugh's Captivity*
as *The Flight of the Eagle,* was adding a passage relating
that some Irish nobles of the Tudor period were losing
their "antique energy and grit" and beginning the decline which in modern Ireland would reduce them to
"fat sheep ready for the butcher," the Financial Relations Commission of the British Government was pre-
paring a report on the two nations' relative monetary
contributions to the maintenance of the Empire since
the Union. The report declared that Ireland had been

overtaxed for years, by more than two million pounds
per year. O'Grady, though a Unionist, was not a "West
Briton"; he was concerned with the welfare of *Ireland*.
Thus this report (some of the findings of which
O'Grady had anticipated in *Toryism and the Tory
Democracy*) seemed to him a godsend: it not only
promised a huge influx of wealth, which would greatly
stimulate the country's economy, but also seemed to
offer a way to heal its serious political and social divisions. Here was one more chance for the landlords *as
a class* to reassert themselves. In an 1897 article
O'Grady, noting that all over Ireland the poor were
holding meetings about the report and asking various
members of the gentry to chair them, interpreted this
movement as evidence that "our poor but sagacious
people perceive that there is a better game a-foot than
that of hunting to ruin their own native Irish aristocracy whom, apart from their national and belligerent
uses, it is hardly worth their while now to hunt any
more for all the flesh, fat, and skin which they still
exhibit." As for the landlords themselves, O'Grady
acknowledged that there was a financial motivation for
them to respond, but he denied that that was their
primary motivation; their interest, he claimed, was
"mainly owing to an awakened public spirit, arising
from a new, generous, and patriotic impulse, and a new
perception of the old law that, as an Aristocracy, they
are the rightful natural leaders, defenders, and champions of this People, who cannot furnish forth such
from their own ranks. This feeling is common enough,
in the minds of the best of our nobility and gentry; it

is a generous and even heroic passion." The use of the word "heroic" here was particularly significant in the light of the associations it held for O'Grady and of his dismissal of that aristocracy as "unheroic" a decade earlier. At the time of this article O'Grady expressed confidence that Ireland would "take" what was coming to her, but gave little attention to the question of the procedure to be used. The following year he published the book *All Ireland*, which took up the question at length.

In the interim between the article and the book, the movement in fact had slowed down. The reasons for this, as O'Grady saw them, were clear: the Irish had not solidified their support fully enough, and then had made the mistake of merely *asking* England to do something to rectify the situation. When England did not immediately act, Irish enthusiasm for the project had received a severe check. Furthermore, he was forced to admit that the landlords, about whom he had written so enthusiastically, had let him down once again. This time they had introduced division into the movement by asking the English for certain alterations in current procedures for dealing with land problems. But O'Grady was still hoping for the best. So in *All Ireland* he urged as a first principle that the entire country should be gotten solidly behind the idea before any further effort was made to deal with England. He was particularly concerned with involving Ulster, where so far there had been comparatively little support for the movement; and he also suggested involving the Highland Scots. In addition, he proposed that as a way

of insuring greater interest among the poorer classes in
Ireland the movement should have as one of its de-
mands the abolition of taxes on tea and tobacco. Finally,
the aristocracy, to whom he made yet another eloquent
appeal, would have to put aside their own narrow class
interests. When nation-wide involvement had been
secured, an All-Ireland Convention would be held.
That Convention would in turn convey specific legislative proposals to the Irish Members in Parliament.
As O'Grady saw it, the Irish Members, voting together
and having the support of the current Opposition party
and a number of independent Members, could not be
outvoted. He was, however, not so naive as to think
that this fact automatically insured success. In an allegorical chapter entitled "The Veiled Player" he warned
of the possibility that England, when confronted with
the seemingly inevitable necessity of reparation would
cast aside the rules and respond with suppression. In
language which might have been that of a Fenian—and
in fact O'Grady has been called a "Fenian Unionist"—
he concluded his argument with the maxim that "the
Imperial Parliament, in its dealings with Ireland, never
yields to Justice, but always to Force." Although the
attainment of the goal would be far from easy, O'Grady
managed to make himself so sanguine once more that
he could write in this volume that "the heroic age of
Ireland is not a tradition, but a prophecy; unfulfilled,
but which is to be fulfilled." Once again his optimism
was to prove unjustified.

At about this time O'Grady, who was a principal
lead-writer for the Dublin *Express,* resigned that posi-

tion and took over the *Kilkenny Moderator*, apparently hoping to use it as a propaganda organ for his idea. He seems to have lost this paper as the result of a libel suit. Undaunted, he founded in 1900 a weekly paper called the *All Ireland Review*. The very name of the new journal reflected his political dream of a few years before, and the first issue inaugurated a series of editorials in which he dealt with that dream and with the reality. By this time it was clear to him that the Irish were not going to respond as he had urged to the Report of the Financial Relations Commission, and furthermore he thought he had at long last discovered why. The title of his series was "The Great Enchantment," a reference to part of the Ulster Cycle of legends. According to the myth, the goddess Macha had been forced, while pregnant, to engage in a race with a chariot; at the end of the race she gave birth, and in her anger she put a curse on the Ultonians, ordaining that whenever their land was threatened with serious danger they would all become subject to pangs and weakness like those of a woman in childbirth. From the curse she exempted only women, children, and—significantly—Cú Chulainn. O'Grady found here an explanation for all of Ireland's troubles: in periods of crisis a mental and spiritual debility fell over the whole country, apparently because of some past guilt. He was careful to include all classes, but obviously he was still particularly concerned with the landlords, whom he now memorably described as failing from the land "while innumerable eyes are dry." During the series of articles he brought up his old hope that if they could not be saved as a class, at least some individuals might be directed towards the right path, and he even reprinted portions of his earlier addresses on the whole subject. But the old enthusiasm was no longer there. He was looking for an equivalent to Cú Chulainn, for an exempt force that could rescue the country from its peril. During this same year he wrote that Cú Chulainn "is not dead at all. He is awake and alive today. He is the genius of the land and race; immortal and unconquerable." Then in 1903 the Wyndham Act provided for mass land purchase on terms favorable to both landlords and tenants, and the end which he had foreseen was at hand. Consequently a gradual shift of interest is discernible in later years as O'Grady, who for all his love of the landlord class loved the country itself more, began to look elsewhere for the means of its salvation. At a time in life when the beliefs of most men have long previously taken their final form, he was able to alter his radically and seek that means in the peasant and working classes whom he had always considered incapable of governing their own destinies, let alone those of the country. The scheme he had proposed in *Toryism and the Tory Democracy* of enlightened aristocrats functioning as heads of little labor colonies reappeared in a new form as he advocated communistic agricultural programs in *The Peasant* and Guild Socialism in A. R. Orage's *The New Age.* Neither ever became an important force in Ireland, and so from O'Grady's own point of view his long political crusade was a failure. But it did have a positive side in its impact upon the modern Irish imagination. In his autobiography Yeats recalled that many men had come to "repeat to themselves like poets' rhymes" certain famous passages from his political writings, and he also suggested the larger significance of O'Grady's work in this area: "all around us people talked or wrote for victory's sake, and were hated for their victories—but here was a man whose rage was a swan-song over all that he had held most dear, and to whom for that very reason every Irish imaginative writer owed a portion of his soul." Yeats himself was in fact one of the chief debtors in this regard.

Yeats's remarks in this passage also introduce the larger issue of O'Grady's connection with and his contribution to the "Irish Literary Renaissance." O'Grady has been hailed by Boyd as "the father of the Literary Revival in Ireland," and this tribute had the most impressive support of Yeats's own assertion that the *History of Ireland* "started us all." While there is a large measure of truth in these statements, they do claim too much: O'Grady's role *was* a major one, but needs to be seen in perspective; there were other forces at work.

The single most significant effect of O'Grady's early books was the revelation to the young men and women of the 1880s and 1890s of their impressive national heritage. Reading his *History* was for many writers the same sort of conversion experience that O'Halloran's book had been for him. Secondarily, he helped open up a whole new vein of subject-matter ideal for a new *Irish* literature: intensely "national" but long predating party controversy and thus appealing to Unionist and Nationalist alike. As early as 1887 an obscure writer named W. C. Upton had borrowed copiously from the *History* for a closet drama on Cú Chulainn, and Yeats and others began to make specific use of him at about the same time: the literary use of Irish legendary materials soon became one of the dominant characteristics of the "Renaissance." The Tudor and political books that followed the *History* produced less spectacular results, but reinforced its effect upon the budding movement.

O'Grady was not, however, a solitary voice. Sir Samuel Ferguson had been seeking literary methods of treating the old legends years before O'Grady's first volume, and other anticipations can be found as early as Tom Moore. Even the poets of the Young Ireland school, though their aims were more political than literary, helped prepare the foundations for the development of a national literature by their creation of a strong national consciousness. But the most important contribution of all was that made by Yeats himself with important assistance from John O'Leary. Yeats met the old Fenian exile in 1885, was converted by him to the cause of *Irish* literature, and then became the guiding force in contemporary writing activities, giving cohesiveness and direction to the vague impulses which were in the air. The literary ideals that he formulated included a working conception of precisely what Irish "national" literature should be: resisting the pressures of political expediency on one hand and provincialism on the other, he called for writing that would be Irish

in subject and spirit but not necessarily politically
Nationalistic (a position that made it possible to include O'Grady's work under the rubric) or isolated
from the influence of the great literary traditions of
other countries. He valued foreign influences especially
in the area of artistic craftsmanship, a quality which
had been woefully lacking in too much nineteenth-
century Irish literature. As particularly important
native subject matter he stressed legend, folklore, and
the "spiritual life." A tireless literary experimenter
himself, he pioneered in the use of such materials and
in the development of viable forms for expressing them.
His position on these matters owed much to O'Leary,
who although a radical Nationalist politically knew
that patriotism alone could never make good art, and
who made available to the young Yeats his own out-
standing collection of Irish books and may even have
been responsible for setting him to reading O'Grady.
In addition to giving these ideals concrete illustration
in his own increasingly prominent creative work, he
strove diligently to spread them to others in more
direct ways. With a steady stream of articles and reviews he propagandized for the ideals and for writers
who adhered to them and defended the nascent movement against such critics as Gavan Duffy, who wanted
only "patriotic" writing, and famous Irish Shakespear-
ean scholar Edward Dowden, who preferred the literature of England and the Continent to anything his
own country might produce. (O'Grady himself entered
this latter controversy, which took place in the pages
of the *Express,* on the side of the new Irish movement.)

As editor of a variety of anthologies Yeats featured the work of the new authors and of those earlier writers who had prepared the way for them. He was also instrumental in founding Irish literary societies in Dublin and London, organizations which had the important function of giving a sense of *group* effort, of a real *movement* in progress. Great as it was, O'Grady's contribution to the beginning of the "Renaissance" cannot be compared to Yeats's. In O'Grady's case there was not in fact any conscious effort to inaugurate such a movement.

Once begun, however, the movement did need an "ancestor," and while still in mid-career O'Grady was elevated to that position. How firmly he came to occupy it can be seen in a humorous episode involving Yeats's "Notes" to the early volumes of his poetry. In an 1899 note to "The Secret Rose" Yeats said he had "founded the man 'who drove the gods out of their Liss,' or fort, upon something I have read about Caolte after the battle of Gabra, when almost all his companions were killed, driving the gods out of their Liss, either at Osraighe, now Ossory, or at Eas Ruaidh, now Asseroe, a waterfall at Ballyshannon, where Ilbreac, one of the children of the goddess Danu, had a Liss. I am writing away from most of my books, and have not been able to find the passage; but I certainly read it somewhere." In revising this passage nearly a decade later Yeats had sought to be more specific about his source, and had looked for the incident, unsuccessfully, in Lady Gregory's *Gods and Fighting Men*. This led him to theorize that "maybe I only read it in Mr. Standish

O'Grady, who has a fine imagination. . . ." Yeats
apparently did not bother to look in *O'Grady* for the
story, for if he had he would have discovered that it
was not there; he simply assumed that O'Grady *would*
have been his source in those days. Actually he had
found the legend in *Silva Gadelica,* an 1892 volume
of translations by O'Grady's cousin Standish Hayes
O'Grady (who was also a relative of Lady Gregory).
Despite the similarity of names Yeats was not confusing
the two men, for the compiler of *Silva Gadelica,* an
accomplished Gaelic scholar, was not known for his
imaginative power and would not have been thought
likely to improvise upon the old texts; Yeats was so
amused at the pedantic stiltedness often characteristic
of his translations that he recalled examples of it years
later. As a final irony, in an even later revision of these
notes he added a phrase attributing *another* image in
the poem to O'Grady, and this time he was correct!

Although O'Grady had thus become almost a mythi-
cal figure during the development of the "Renaissance,"
his active involvement with it and his contributions
to it did not cease. That they did not was in fact partly
due to Yeats himself. He had started later than
O'Grady, but soon became a more marketable writer
and had far more practical connections in literary matters. Because he valued O'Grady's work so highly he
made a determined effort to keep him associated with
the movement, to provide him with opportunities to
write, and to create an audience for him. It was Yeats
who got *The Bog of Stars* into the New Irish Library,
and in a brief autobiographical fragment O'Grady

made his own acknowledgment that the enthusiasm of Yeats and others for the *History* had caused London publishers to be interested in his other books. Yeats personally reviewed several of O'Grady's new productions with lavish praise and included practically all of his work in his lists of "Best Irish Books." When attacked for having done the latter, he firmly defended his position: "I could do no more than give Mr. O'Grady the lion's share, because his books have affected one more powerfully than those of any other writer. . . . I believe them to be ideal books of their kind, books of genius. . . ." On one occasion he even persuaded AE, who had planned a negative criticism of the method of *All Ireland,* not to take the risk of discouraging him. While Yeats did meet with a fair degree of success in his efforts to aid O'Grady, he later speculated that "if, instead of that one admirable little book *The Bog of Stars,* we had got all his histories and imaginative works into the hands of our young men, he might have brought the imagination of Ireland nearer the Image and the honeycomb."

During the late 'nineties Yeats and AE felt that the dominant feature of contemporary Irish literature was its belief in some sort of spiritual reality underlying the ordinary world. This was obviously an accurate appraisal of their own work, and possibly that of a few other writers. At the time, however, they were prone to seeing this "spiritual" impulse in virtually all their contemporaries. AE especially sought to include O'Grady. In his opinion, though O'Grady's "outer mind" was "simple and unmystical," the "inner being

rested on some fundamental spiritual reality, and clung
to it without ever being able to rationalize his faith."
He was "rather more in sympathy with mystical
thought than he could bring himself to express." AE
discerned such a "spiritual" content in the *History*: he
knew the book well, was aware of O'Grady's modifications of his originals, and claimed O'Grady had made
"the warrior seem almost a divine type" and removed
from battle "the lust of blood" until the "conflicts of
warriors seem not a warring upon flesh and blood, but
the everlasting battle where the Clan Cailitan are the
dark powers and Cuculain the spirit of redeeming
light." To a considerable extent AE was here anach-
ronistically finding his own concerns in O'Grady's
work: during the 'nineties he, as well as Yeats and
William Larminie, had found in books by John Rhys
and Henri d'Arbois de Jubainville scholarly support
for interpretation of several of the old Gaelic legends
as myths of the opposition of light and darkness, good
and evil. AE himself wrote a poem on this subject
entitled "The Everlasting Battle," and a later excised
passage in Yeats's "Fergus and the Druid" had Fergus
feeling "the demons and the gods" waging "an eternal
battle" within him. O'Grady's conscious reasons for
emphasizing the Clan Cailitin may well have been
"aesthetic" ones; but AE in fact claimed no more than
unconscious motivation. There is some scattered support in O'Grady's writings for asserting the existence
of such impulses, but no ordered metaphysic. O'Grady
was at least conscious enough of the current prevalence
of this impulse and of the connection with the "true

voice of Ireland" which both Yeats and AE asserted
for it that in the famous "Slieve Gullion" passage in
The Flight of the Eagle he included among the figures
linked with the holy mountain "some youth wandering
unconsoled, o'erladen with the burthen of his thoughts,
rapt with visions, tormented by the gods." According
to AE, O'Grady said he was thinking specifically of
him.

At the end of the century, when Yeats began realizing
his dream of a native theater, one of his first steps was
to urge O'Grady to write a play. O'Grady did not respond, and remained detached as the theater came into
being and began to flourish. George Moore has given
a rather pathetic picture of O'Grady at this time: hear-
ing his name mentioned at a dinner party, Moore
asked who he was,

and my neighbor drew my attention to a gray, round-
headed man, and after looking at him for some time I
said: "How lonely he seems among all these people! Does
he know anybody? Or is he very unpopular?"
"He is very little read, but we all admire him. He is
our past"; and my neighbor told me that O'Grady had
written passages that for fiery eloquence and energy were
equal to any that I would find in Anglo-Irish literature.
"Only——"
"Only what?" I asked.
And he told me that O'Grady's talent reminded him of
the shaft of a beautiful column rising from amid rubble-
heaps.

However, it is clear from other sources such as the
memoirs of poetess Ella Young that O'Grady was no
mere relic but a presence who could awe and inspire

members of a younger generation. His refusal to accept Yeats's invitation was probably the result of some serious doubts on his part concerning the enterprise; in any event, as the drama movement took shape he became disturbed by the course it was following. During its early years, when romantic and legendary subject-matter was common, he argued that the Irish myths should not be "brought down to the crowd" or Irish ideals might be degraded and the soul of the land banished; but he was himself essentially romantic in taste, and found himself out of sympathy with the realism which soon came to dominate. But if he refused to contribute to the theater, he did in at least one case become a part of it. On February 20, 1900 the theater put on a performance of *The Bending of the Bough,* a revision by George Moore (with some help from Yeats) of a play by Edward Martyn. Its subject was a dispute between Ireland and England over a debt owed by the latter to the former. The Irish have a good claim but are divided among themselves about whether or not to press it; they fail to achieve unity, and do not receive any compensation. Not only was this clearly an allegory of the Financial Relations Report affair (with which Martyn and Moore, both of the landlord class themselves, were quite familiar), but also one of the characters in the play, Ralph Kirwan, is to a large extent based upon O'Grady. It is he who preaches to the young hero the absolute necessity of Ireland's various factions uniting in the common interest over this issue, and who has introduced him to the legendary past and its promise of a great future

for the country. He also talks much of the "spiritual,"
and here the figure of AE seems to blend with that of
O'Grady as model. O'Grady knew the play and saw
its meaning, for in a periodical article he discussed the
character of the young hero and the real person on
whom O'Grady imagined him to be patterned, one of
the few landlords who had responded as O'Grady had
urged during the affair.

While he thus refused to become involved in the
theater movement, O'Grady was during the early years
of its development making a very important practical
contribution to the general growth of the "Renaissance" through his editorship of the *All Ireland Review,*
which he produced almost single-handedly from 1900
to 1907. Since their emergence in the 'eighties the new
Irish writers had had difficulties finding in their own
country organs sympathetic to their ideals and their
work, and at the beginning of the new century the need
for such organs was still great. O'Grady's paper was
open to anyone who wanted to write about Irish subjects, and during its existence its contributors included
Yeats, AE, John Eglinton, Lady Gregory, T. W. Rolleston, John Todhunter, Nora Hopper, Alice Milligan,
Ella Young and many others. It also provided O'Grady
himself with a continually available medium in which
to address the nation on both literary and political
matters, and he published some of his new works in it
and reprinted some of his early ones. Eventually, however, the strain of running it became too much for him
and he had to give it up.

At this period his works began to produce a number

of imitators. It was this group more than O'Grady himself whom Joyce parodied in the "Cyclops" episode of *Ulysses*: their exaggerations of O'Grady's method of idealizing the Irish heroes fit perfectly the technique of "gigantism" which Joyce chose as his medium for the chapter. Joyce was conscious of O'Grady's own work, too, for his picture of the Citizen bears a recognizable resemblance to a passage in *Finn and His Companions* describing Fionn MacCumhail: "his lips and cheeks were smooth, the golden masses of his hair rolled over his wide shoulders. He wore a hugh rough mantle of many skins of wild-boars sewn together; his shirt was of deer-skin laced with leathern thongs; his knees bare, and his mocasins of untanned hairy ox-hide. He carried a great shield and spear. . . ." Joyce's romanticism was of a far different sort than O'Grady's and he could not accept the latter's interpretation of the old legends. It was no accident that the catalogue of Irish heroes and bogus "heroes" in Joyce's book began with Cú Chulainn, whose unnatural ability to expand his own stature O'Grady had found it necessary to omit: in the *Ulysses* passage he stands as an emblem of both real and artificial heroism, of inflation and deflation, and thus epitomizes the mode of the entire episode.

O'Grady's giving up of the *All Ireland Review* marked the end of his organic involvement in contemporary literary activities; he remained in Ireland until 1918—when ill health forced him to seek a warmer climate—but, in the words of his son, "disappeared from the public ken." He died in the Isle of Wight in 1928.

Yet even after the end of the period of organic involvement his works continued to have an impact upon the
movement, not only upon Yeats and AE, who had long
felt his influence, but also to some extent upon younger
writers as well. AE himself was particularly active in
keeping them before this younger group. Austin Clarke
has given a vivid picture of the enthusiasm with which
AE quoted passages from the *History* and leant him
that and several of O'Grady's other books. Significantly,
Clarke, though he could see the causes of AE's own
excitement, did not feel an equally strong emotion;
coming later, he knew the sagas in better versions and
knew the great imaginative works that had since been
based on them. Such factors probably had much to do
with the almost total obscurity into which O'Grady's
work eventually fell.

In those years following the failure of the *All Ireland
Review* O'Grady's influence was felt upon the political
scene as well, through the agency of Padraic Pearse.
O'Grady had been a dedicated Unionist, while Pearse's
Nationalism literally meant more to him than his life,
but the two were linked by the figure of Cú Chulainn.
In 1912 Pearse wrote that "what Ireland wants beyond
all other modern countries, is a new birth of the heroic
spirit," and to the boys of the school he founded he
urged "we must re-create and perpetuate in Ireland
the knightly tradition of Cuchulainn, 'better is short
life with honour than long life with dishonour. . . .' "
By Pearse's time there were many other sources for the
epic materials, but AE has testified to "Pearse's love for
the Cuchulain whom O'Grady discovered or invented."

O'Grady himself was apparently unaware of his connection with Pearse, and might well have been displeased with the linking of his hero to an armed insurrection. On the other hand, Yeats has related that at the same dinner party recorded by Moore, O'Grady later in the evening (and now "very drunk") said to the group that "we have now a literary movement, it is not very important; it will be followed by a political movement, that will not be very important; then must come a military movement, that will be important indeed" and went on to urge that landlords drill the sons of their tenants and bid them "march to the conquest" of England. (Yeats saw O'Grady's militant stance here as an outgrowth of hatred of England for having "used" and then deserted the Irish aristocracy.) But regardless of whether or not he approved of the event itself, there remains the possibility, suggested by AE and others, that O'Grady's books "contributed the first spark of ignition" to the Easter Rising. Conor Cruise O'Brien has convincingly warned against asserting such absolute causal connections, pointing out that the leaders of the revolution had within them a strong vein of romantic nationalism and that this vein was at least as likely to be touched by the mediocre but intensely patriotic poetry of the Young Irelanders and the words of Tone, Emmet, and Mitchel. What can be asserted can be expressed in the terms of Yeats's "The Statues": life sometimes imitates art, and when Pearse summoned Cú Chulainn to his side in the Post Office, the figure that appeared owed its form in part to O'Grady's work. And O'Grady himself would certainly have been moved by "The Statues," for its vision of a new Ireland taking the ancient Ulster hero as its presiding inspiration had been his own over half a century before. The nobility of the vision has not been diminished by its failure to find realization in contemporary Ireland.

O'Grady's work, never widely read even in his own country, has been practically unknown elsewhere; yet at least indirectly he has had an importance transcending the merely parochial. His role in the emergence and growth of the "Irish Renaissance" was a significant one, and that movement can now be seen as one of the most splendid achievements of twentieth-century literature in English; through Yeats and its other major figures he has made a considerable impact. In the future he may receive some of the recognition he merits but which he himself, being a shy and retiring man, never sought. Until then he must remain a fascinating but too little known figure in modern literary history.

Bibliography

I. WORKS BY STANDISH JAMES O'GRADY

History of Ireland: The Heroic Period. London: Sampson Low, Searle, Marston, and Rivington; and Dublin: E. Ponsonby, 1878.

Early Bardic Literature, Ireland. London: Sampson Low, Searle, Marston, and Rivington; and Dublin: E. Ponsonby, 1879.

History of Ireland: Cuculain and his Contemporaries. London: Sampson Low, Searle, Marston, and Rivington; and Dublin: E. Ponsonby, 1880.

History of Ireland: Critical and Philosophical. London: Sampson Low and Co.; and Dublin: E. Ponsonby and Co., 1881.

The Crisis in Ireland. Dublin: E. Ponsonby; and London: Simpkin and Marshall, 1882.

Cuculain: An Epic. London: Sampson, Low, Searle, Marston, and Rivington; and Dublin: E. Ponsonby, 1882.

Toryism and the Tory Democracy. London: Chapman and Hall, Ltd., 1886.

Red Hugh's Captivity. London: Ward and Downey, 1889.

Finn and His Companions. London: T. Fisher Unwin, 1892.

The Bog of Stars. London: T. Fisher Unwin; Dublin: Sealy, Bryers and Walker; and New York: P. J. Kennedy, 1893.

The Story of Ireland. London: Methuen and Co., 1894.

The Coming of Cuculain. London: Methuen and Co., 1894.

Lost on Du-Corrig. London, Paris, and Melbourne: Cassell and Company, 1894.

The Chain of Gold. London: T. Fisher Unwin, 1895.

In the Wake of King James. London: J. M. Dent and Co., 1896.

Ulrick the Ready. London: Downey and Co., 1896.

The Flight of the Eagle. London: Lawrence and Bullen, 1897.

All Ireland. Dublin: Sealy, Bryers, and Walker; and London: T. Fisher Unwin, 1898.

The Queen of the World. London: Lawrence and Bullen, Ltd., 1900.

In the Gates of the North. Kilkenny: Standish O'Grady, 1901.

Hugh Roe O'Donnell. Belfast: Nelson and Knox, Ltd., 1902.

The Masque of Finn. Dublin: Sealy, Bryers and Walker, 1907.

The Triumph and Passing of Cuculain. Dublin: The Talbot Press; and London: T. Fisher Unwin, 1920.

Standish O'Grady: Selected Essays and Passages, ed. Ernest A. Boyd. Dublin: Talbot Press, n.d.

NOTE: none of these books is currently in print, but the Talbot Press Ltd of Dublin will be publishing during 1970 a new edition of *Finn and His Companions.*

II. SECONDARY STUDIES

Boyd, Ernest A. *Appreciations and Depreciations.* New York: John Lane Co., 1918.

————. *Ireland's Literary Renaissance.* New York: John Lane Co., 1916.

Clarke, Austin. *A Penny in the Clouds.* London: Routledge and Kegan Paul, 1968.

Marcus, Phillip L. *Yeats and the Beginning of the Irish Renaissance*. Ithaca: Cornell University Press, 1970.

O'Conor, Norreys Jephson. *Changing Ireland*. Cambridge: Harvard University Press, 1924.

O'Grady, Hugh Art. *Standish James O'Grady: The Man and the Work*. Dublin and Cork: the Talbot Press, 1929.

Rolleston, C. H. *Portrait of an Irishman*. London: Methuen and Co., 1939.

Russell, George. "Standish O'Grady," in *Irish Literature*, ed. Justin McCarthy (Chicago: deBower-Elliot Co., 1904), VII, 2737–2740.

Thompson, William Irwin. *The Imagination of an Insurrection*. New York: Oxford University Press, 1967.

Yeats, W. B. *Autobiographies*. London: Macmillan, 1966.

————. "Battles Long Ago," *Bookman*, February, 1895, p. 153.

————. "Mr. Standish O'Grady's 'Flight of the Eagle,'" *Bookman*, August, 1897, pp. 123–124.